MW00743535

ISBN 0-634-09174-3

7777 W. BLUEMOUND RD. P.O. BOX 13819 MILWAUKEE, WI 53213

Visit Hal Leonard Online at
www.halleonard.com

CONTENTS

TOO MUCH OF A GOOD THING

Words and Music by
ALAN JACKSON

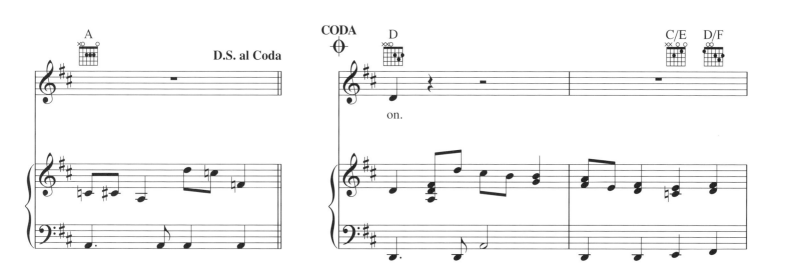

Yeah, we've got __ a good __ thing __ go - in' on.

RAINY DAY IN JUNE

Words and Music by
ALAN JACKSON

to help me dry ___ my eyes. ___
on the wrong side of ___ the bed. ___

And I need a blue ___ sky
And on ___ the right ___ side

o - ver - head ___
laid a note. ___

so

I can clear ___ my mind. ___
I knew what ___ it said. ___

12

I see ___ your face ___ in ev - 'ry cloud ___ that pass -

- es ___ on this rain - y day ___ in June. ___

D.S. al Coda

CODA

rit.

USA TODAY

Words and Music by
ALAN JACKSON

IF LOVE WAS A RIVER

Words and Music by ADAM WRIGHT
and SHANNON WRIGHT

IF FRENCH FRIES WERE FAT FREE

Words and Music by
ALAN JACKSON

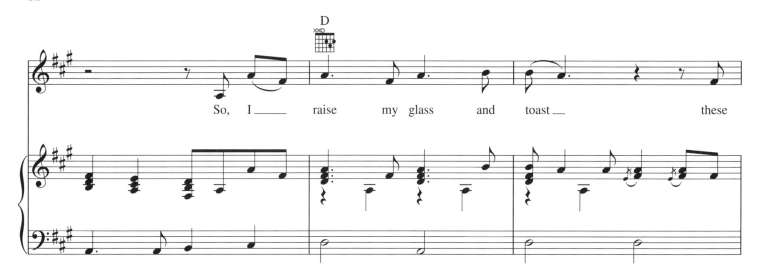

So, I ___ raise my glass and toast ___ these

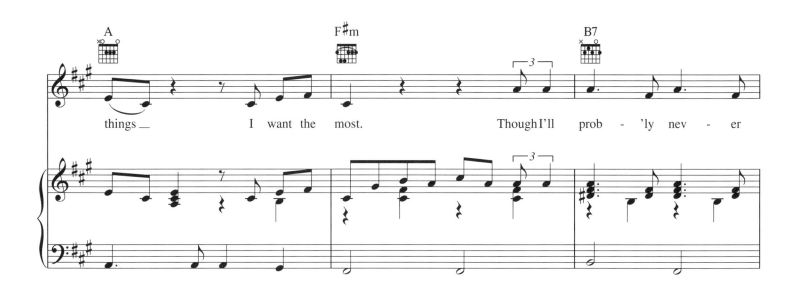

things ___ I want the most. Though I'll prob - 'ly nev - er

D.S. al Coda

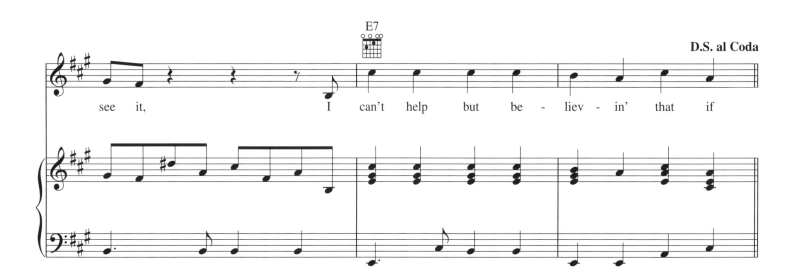

see it, I can't help but be - liev - in' that if

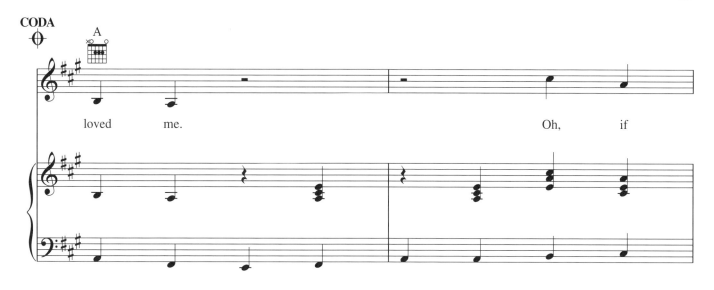

loved me.   Oh,   if

french ____ fries ____ were fat free   and you still ____

loved   me. ____

YOU DON'T HAVE TO PAINT ME A PICTURE

Words and Music by
ALAN JACKSON

D.S. al Coda

CODA

wall.   Yeah, I can see the

writ - ing   on the wall. _____

rit.

THERE YA GO

Words and Music by DAN HILL
and KEITH STEGALL

So,   just   hold   on   tight.

Put one

THE TALKIN' SONG REPAIR BLUES

Words and Music by
DENNIS LINDE

STRONG ENOUGH

Words and Music by
ADAM WRIGHT

you don't ____ make ____ the wine.

Mex - i - co, ____ you don't ____ make ____ te -

qui - la ____ strong e - nough ____ to

get her ____ off my ____ mind,

MONDAY MORNING CHURCH

Words and Music by ERIN ENDERLIN
and BRENT BAXTER

BURNIN' THE HONKY TONKS DOWN

Words and Music by SHAWN CAMP
and BILLY BURNETTE

Fast Bluegrass

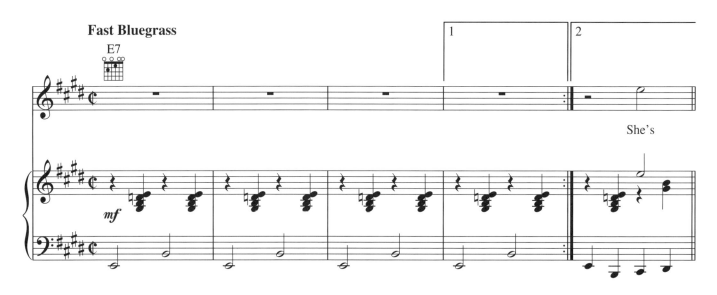

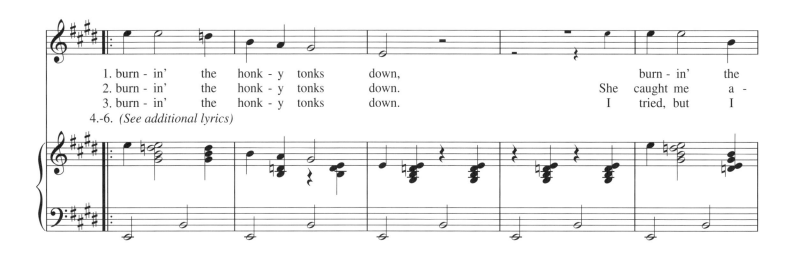

1. burn-in' the honk-y tonks down,   burn-in' the
2. burn-in' the honk-y tonks down.   She caught me a-
3. burn-in' the honk-y tonks down.   I tried, but I
4.-6. *(See additional lyrics)*

honk-y tonks down. __   Smoke's been a-ris-in'
run-nin' a-round. __   She was danc-in' in the ash-es when they
could-n't put 'em out. __   Did my best to save the whis-key, but the

all o - ver town. She's burn - in' the honk - y tonks down.
caught her with them match - es. She's burn - in' the honk - y tonks down.
flame was just too risk - y. She's burn - in' the honk - y tonks down.

Instrumental ad lib.

1-5

6

She's

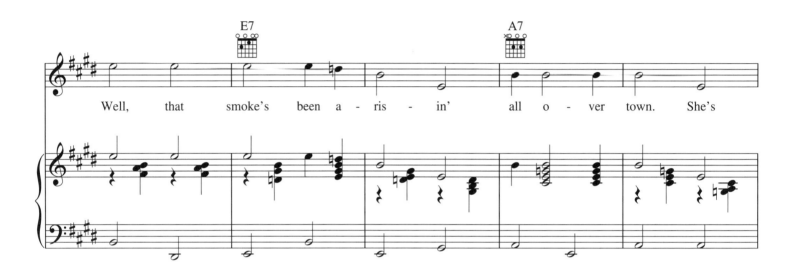

Well, that smoke's been a - ris - in' all o - ver town. She's

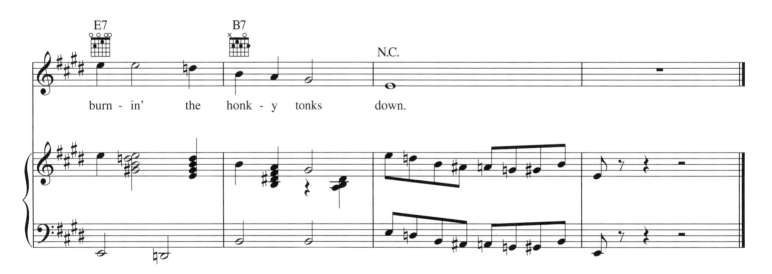

burn - in' the honk - y tonks down.

Additional Lyrics

4. She's burnin' the honky tonks down.
   She couldn't stop that honky tonk sound.
   It was sizzlin' like a griddle when I ran out with my fiddle.
   She's burnin' the honky tonks down.

5. She's burnin' the honky tonks down.
   She's down in the jail house now.
   Said she's felt no remorse for breakin' out that torch.
   She's burnin' the honky tonks down.

6. She's burnin' the honky tonks down.
   Burnin' the honky tonks down.
   Smoke's been a-risin' all over town.
   She's burnin' the honky tonks down.

TO DO WHAT I DO

Words and Music by
TIM JOHNSON